Cursing Bagels

ALFRED BRENDEL

Cursing Bagels

English versions by the author
with Richard Stokes

faber and faber

First published in 2004
by Faber and Faber Limited
3 Queen Square London WC1N 3AU

Photoset by Wilmaset Ltd, Wirral
Printed in England by T. J. International Ltd, Padstow, Cornwall

A CIP record for this book
is available from the British Library

ISBN 0-571-22070-3

10 9 8 7 6 5 4 3 2 1

Contents

Cursing Bagels

We shall now turn our attention
to the lyric big bang
the ear-splitting source
of countless lyric galaxies

Which means we have to bear in mind
that any particular big bang
is bound to be
only one of many conceivable
if not perfectly plausible
big bangs
within a bottomless lyric universe

Which means it should be taken into account
that each of these big bangs
must hurl universal
albeit diverse
if not downright incompatible
laws of poetics
into orbit

Which means it ought to be acknowledged
that each of those universally relevant strictures
already contains its own negation
Which ultimately means
that even the most affectionate poem
whether free-wheeling or prosodic
may be classified as an echo
of cosmic catastrophe

Almighty initiator
old warmonger
cornucopia of kindliness and bliss
monster supreme
celestial penis cosmic womb
lowest common denominator
eye that sees all and perceives nothing
you hide
shine in absentia
Music Minus One
scale minus tonic
variations without a theme
salt without soup
maw without tongue
But fear not
we remain loyal
look up to you
our creation
as if you were hovering above
heap abuse on you alone
our lethal ozone hole
our personal tailor-made chaos
the stirring of a butterfly
in the jungle

No one believes me
yet I can only repeat
It wasn't I
who killed your hamster
the doves in the dovecot
the sheep beneath your window
the magpies and moles
the cyclist on the road
the beggar staring at your house
the woman in your arms
mother father
not I
who winked at you in the mirror
You're next

Whether he had been born
remained open to question
He himself did not recall the event
and one refrained
from trusting others
Perhaps he had existed
long before he noticed
a cuckoo's egg
planted in his parents' nest
a botched demiurge
marooned in this existence
unlaunched
and
who knows
unending

There won't ever be another Death
In overwhelming numbers
we abolished it
snuffing out volcanoes
banishing storms to the stratosphere
deflecting plagues onto those
who incorrigibly persist
in taking our lives
Clad in armour
we face them
with lidless eyes

Surrounded by all that noise
let us be silent
No chance
even to hear one's own voice
A few gestures will do
arms flung above our heads
mouth pulled down in comic despair
When no one's looking
we hastily touch each other
What could be lovelier
than wordless touching
From your lips
I can read your tiny sighs
your inaudible scream

There is something between us
It sneaked in
unnoticed
turning our heads towards each other
directing our eyes
across the room
into the other's eyes
until they kindle
radiate
yet open on an inner darkness
into which we plunge
our eyes dazzled
while the phantom between us
the perfect puppeteer
draws our strings together
for a fleeting moment of truth

Merely expanding won't do
let us taper ourselves as well
be rarefied
even evaporate
without a trace

By all means consolidate
but don't fail simultaneously to dissolve
liquefy
a minute drizzle

The most sophisticated way
of speaking softly
is silence

(To Jean Paul)

There are ideas
which spread as rapidly as waterlilies
but waterlilies remain waterlilies
Ideas however
get grimy
weather-beaten
and fade like mirrors
losing their lustre
going blind

Others cling to survival
changeable as April weather
squinting in all directions at once

While the most lethal
dazzle unremittingly
feeding on people

The gallows-bird
at sunset
sits astride his gallows
and sings
not overly melodious
no match for the blackbird or the nightingale
but mightily expressive
con somma espressione
fervent like a circular saw
whose motor suddenly cuts out
when darkness
pulls the noose

As soon as the virtual people
decided to behave like you and me
we knew
our game was up
There they sit
too sleek of face for our comfort
pour their tea
look languidly into each other's eyes
or collapse laughing
Impeccably
yet with notable refinement
they play the piano
procreate discreetly next door
and shoot the pigeons from the roof
while we
veterans of normality
see no way out
but to mutate into angels
or even better
turn horrendously evil

Devils' pageant

1

There they go again
whooshing up
to ram their cute little horns
into our bosoms
provided our bosoms are big enough to flaunt
or be tickled by their horns
making us wet ourselves
till
all that's left of us
is a puddle
in which they splash around
like little kids
Who'd have thought
devils
capable of such behaviour

2

On Monday morning
Stechbein arrives to mess up the tuning
on Tuesday
he hides the pedals
on Wednesday
he pours collodium over the strings
on Thursday
he covers the keys with glue
on Friday
he guzzles the hammers
on Saturday
he sets the case on fire
on Sunday

he gets drunk with Weinstay
Even piano devils
have their day off

3
Big devils
Behemoths Ahrimans
merely block the water-pipes
or get stuck in the chimney
The fire-brigade
removes them routinely
while the small anonymous ones
carry on their business unhampered
Well-nigh invisible
they nestle in your eardrum
nibble at your joints
or rattle through your thorax
House-trained devils
are sought-after dinner guests
Smiling coyly
they ogle the hostess
with their yellow eyes

4
By now
they'd come to adore him
rejoicing
whenever a close-up of his teeth
filled the TV screen
Waiting our turn to be devoured
we stand in line
shivering with fear
though it must be admitted

he only consumes half of us
some lyrical urge
keeps him from finishing the job
this
in all fairness
we should consider
when watching him
trim his tirades
and sharpen his teeth
Engines running
the ambulances outside
stand ready to rush off with our remains
howling through town
while the nurses
eager for our autograph
inject us against lockjaw and rabies
A few weeks or years later
we return to our work-place
Steinway & Sons
a toupée on our head
one leg in a splint
To hell with the left pedal

5
When devils feel bored
they play at being good
With pious faces
hands neatly folded
they sit round the boardroom table
and forgive each other anything they ever did
or might be itching to do
The first to dissolve in tears
wins

6

Demons
scarcely distinguishable from gods
play on the furrows of our souls
like instrumentalists
painfully but with panache
When they squeeze us
we whine
like dogs craving to get out
to bark at the dark
Dog-like
we'd love to bite them
our tormentors
only to find ourselves
biting our own tongues

7

No it wasn't the cook
and don't let's blame the gardener
still less the lady's maid
least of all Griffiths
the butler
despite his haggard look
On no account
should we consider the corgies
who have
admittedly
mutilated a number of toddlers before
As for the farm manager
a self-declared gipsy
he had joined his family for dinner
in their caravan
miles away

Finally
any personal involvement of our host
may safely be discounted
since His Lordship is equipped
with only one leg
A statue in the vegetable garden
will remind us for ever
of the sorry affair

8
The news
that the devil does not
actually exist
was relayed to us
by none other
than the devil himself
Duly saddened
we have pondered this fact
and decided henceforth
to advertise our own hell

9
Gondolas
lie scattered upside down
like stranded whales
Black smoke
billows from the rooftops
The dome of Santa Maria Maggiore sinks moaning
into the lagoon
One final explosion
rips apart the Doge's Palace
Swept along by the flood
rodents

the size of tomcats
paddle about inside San Marco
and bite the clerics
who struggle to salvage what's left of their Saint
When all is over
Mario Praz
the master of ceremonies
faces himself in the mirror
ready for the duel
of evil eyes

One needs to coax them in
Angels like to be asked
First of all
you have to precisely
imagine their looks
clawed feet
one white one black wing
red eyeballs
the sweetness of their voice
The moment I hear that voice
I know it has arrived
Opening my eyes
I see it looks exactly
the way I imagined
the shape
of a superhuman hen
the discreet hunchback
the fluent German
its aura
Couldn't possibly be a devil
devils have lost their aura
as anyone knows
Come sweet Angel
I sing
and betray your secret
$2 \times 2 = 13$
says the Angel

In Heaven's Telecom
angels man the switchboard
Plugging and unplugging
they crouch there
wings bristling
The system
an early installation
is antiquated
When God cranks the handle
there is a roar on the line
connections
are cut off abruptly
Off and on
you catch a distorted voice
must be the Boss
unmistakable those squawking sounds
No one can guess what he's on about
It's clear to all though
that he's swearing
Aren't angels easier
right next to your ear
they sigh
and talk love

The angel of reason
does not protect us
Wherever it treads
tall grass grows
Whoever it touches
spreads out his arms
and flies
with eyes wide open
for five minutes
through filtered air
Its voice tells us
that's not what you are
Any resemblance
is mere delusion

The angel of self-deceit
the avenger angel
the angel of absolute truth
the angel of total recall
the angel of selective oblivion
the angel of unrequited love
the laughing angel
the angel of health (organic)
the angel of lost innocence
the mouse angel
Pegasus
Chimera
the changel strangel derangel
the flying sausage
the angel of hullaballoo
the scavenger angel

Since the angels
can no longer be kept at bay
we implore the County Council
to rid us of this nuisance
Like rabbits they multiply
those celestial things
while the authorities
contrive to look the other way
For a start
we'd suggest the extermination of Baroque putti
followed
one by one
by a Swedenborg embargo
a Rilke boycott
and a Handke-Wenders quarantine
Only on behalf of Raphael's cherubs
would we plead for mercy
after all
it was mummy
who nailed them above our bed
By now
even higher beings have earned the right
to be treated like you and me
Disguised as pigeons
shouting AUGUSTA
swashbuckling
and copulating
they people rooftops and balconies
It should be evident
even to the RSPCA
that swift action is needed

The day comes
        when the angel
                grabs the toy trumpet
                and blows
                        us adults

                                    away

Strutting up and down the aisle
as though on a footbridge
angels by Giotto Piero and Angelico
parade in aeroplanes
living proof of the loss of heaven
Rustling past Arabs and Texans
they brush us with their wings
majestic
if not bowed and humbled
while cherubs climb all over the ladies
and Ginevra de' Benci
heavenly
yet remarkably tough
perches on my knee
in blue and green

The inner angel
somewhat constricted
in its quandary
what more can it achieve
than shine through our eyes
or touch our heart
In fact
it would sooner loosen its limbs (outside)
flutter a bit
float (up there)
if not fly around unfettered
(a dot in the sky)
go into a spin
loop the loop
an accomplished stunt-flier
watched by us
down here
with awe

before it alights
next to us
acknowledges the applause
and
with a grimace
slips back inside

You may not have noticed
but lately
angels are everywhere
popes pianists policemen
even chickens
nothing but angels
giraffes assassins lapdogs
tortoises cricketers
all angels
if not archangels
flapping along
announcing
blurting out hymns
in MY honour

Don't count on me
my angelic brood
Leave me alone
I despise you
To hell with you
you servile godly lot

The moment I turn away
they start rebelling

Once a year
as hell and heaven open their gates
devils and angels
join in playing the human game
Foregoing old family feuds
they fraternize
fool around
mock God and Satan
and whirr like mating cockchafers
double-decker style
through earth's orbit
At the end of the day
when Gabriel summons the winged armies
back to their garrisons
they struggle
disoriented
to recall whence they came
or where they belong

Where
these days
is the seat
of the soul
In the buttocks you say
Balderdash
that's where I sit
No one squashes their soul by sitting on it
It's surely the soul
that has to sit
and fit
like a Savile Row suit
like false teeth
safely installed
a stable soul
that doesn't shift around
like mine
from the pineal gland
into the lungs
from the stomach
into the kidneys
one more push
What the devil
is it up to
the soul down there

The idea
to marry myself
took hold of me
the moment Victor and his spouse
yelled at each other
during a performance
by the local brass band
of Vivaldi's Seasons
With blinding clarity
epiphany set in
Next to the mirror
I nodded to myself
lips pursed into a kiss
Being all yours
I told myself
at one with yourself
available to oneself at all hours
this state of grace
should make life worth living
During the wedding march
I strode
in kilt and tie
all by myself
hand in hand with myself
a twofold yes on my lips
For months to come
ecstasy held sway
I lived a dream
read every wish from my eyes
bedded myself on roses
whispered
all to myself

terms of endearment
When offered
by the Max Planck Institute
to have myself cloned
I declined
Self-contained love
was what I stood for
Meanwhile
people grin at me on the street
fans send me email
in TV debates
I plead for the minimal family
Later this evening
I've got a date
It's about time
to cuckold myself

From all directions
they fly
burrowing into tree-trunks
thwacking into rooftops
or hopping like birds along the balcony

Like reddish snails
they peer out of flower-beds
creep up house walls
or adorn
horrendously puffed up
the soccer pitch
a landscape of blue-veined hilltops

Solemnly
we enter their elongated orifices
step multi-nostrilled
into purple cathedrals
and sniff around
before
felled by the olfactory burden
we block the respiratory ducts
like small pink adenoids

How he grew and grew
the little fellow
till he became an elephant's trunk
In elephant style
it reaches out
proffers itself to passers-by
begging
or spraying them like a garden hose
Happily he trumpets away
lifts an abandoned car from the ditch
and steals ladies' handbags
knowing full well
that ladies always carry chocolate
Smeared with brown and smacking his lips
he huddles up
and sleeps
invisible now
a dreamless sleep

When Emil visits me
he quickly grows peckish
Even as he dictates his first lines
he gazes in my direction
smiling self-consciously
before he sinks his teeth in
Emil has sharp teeth
Between mouthfuls
he continues his dictation
Once in a while
he digresses
flashing his burgundy-red dentures
before diving down once more
with a hiss

The general is my lover
His pockets are full of jewels
when I pick out a gold tooth
he pulls a face

The general is severe yet just
At home
he plays his violin
pats his paunch
decorates me with his medals

The general and I eat oysters
Plagued by lumbago
he'd miss manoeuvres
I am the plague

The general does several things at once
While practising octaves
he plans the next war
Critics
praise his beguiling tone

When Einstein
having arrived in Heaven
saw God throwing dice
he turned about and said
To Hell

In Plotzk on the Vistula
the devil
visible to all and sundry
appeared on January 5 1809
and laid
as Ernst Theodor Amadeus Hoffmann had anticipated
his tail over everything

Up and down
Up and down
rides the Almighty
in the elevator
of all elevators
on rainy weekends

To demonstrate our unity
we shall play
with one finger
the one note
that unites us
once

Once upon a time
I was no wunderkind
Due to my obstinacy
though
I became one later
No easy task
stretching yourself
yet remaining under five foot six
for the sailor-suit still to fit
Lately
it was on my 97th birthday
the Ham and High wrote
he performs
we are pleased to report
like a ten-year-old

I'd say
it was worth it

Here he sits
beckoning
with his arthritic hand
that can no longer hold a baton
Pray
fetch those tapes from the archives
switch on the machine
Rosenkavalier Met 1974
No not the trio
just the applause
the volume appropriately loud
For nineteen minutes
I raised the roof
Then the recordings from Salzburg and Paris
gales of public esteem
Paris as always the loudest
Salzburg the longest
a full ten minutes longer than Nikisch
People wept
whoever does that today
sobbed and pummelled each other
outside my dressing-room
The lady
who forced herself in during the interval
in Buenos Aires of all places
and exposed herself
managed to break a rib
during our embrace
For months on end
the whole town clamoured
to inspect her midriff
They loved me

no doubt about that
even the musicians
ate from my hand
When I gouged out
the leader's right eye
with my stick
the good man
offered me his left
The nastier I became
the better they played
something Bruno Walter
would never have pulled off
Finally
Fidelio from Budapest
an acoustical quirk
you can actually hear
how
in the general pandemonium
the pretty usherette
after handing me flowers on stage
fell unconscious
into the orchestra pit

The man in the front row
steadily scratching himself
has he actually come
to hear Adalbert Brennettle
the greatest falsetto of any gender
our Adalbert
alias Albino
because he's red-eyed

When Adalbert stares
his look pierces us
somewhere between heart and marrow
and lingers there
nettling us
But we also came
to hear his screeching portamenti
his semiquavers
which he aims at us
like machine-gun fire
his mezza voce
for which he closes both eyes

When he opens them again
we shudder
Now he fastens his gaze
on the man in the front row
whose face turns redder and redder
as he crawls under his seat
scratching himself furiously
nettled forever

In the hereafter
we can make up
for all we missed in life
Beethoven for example
can be retrieved over there
as a baker
With his customary fury
he hurls the dough into the oven
The resemblance of his sonata movements to pretzels
was first remarked upon by Tovey
but it was Schenker's acute ear
that likened the late bagatelles
to poppy-seed cake
The deceased master's most recent creation
his 'Cursing Bagels'
curse
when you sink your teeth into them

The urge to sing hymns
has recently
caught on amongst bank-robbers
With stentorian voices
they praise God
while the cashier sinks to her knees
and the bank manager
chiming in
turns out his pockets

That pianos
should not merely be cooked
but also smoked
has recently been discovered
by pure chance
A fire in the local piano store
surprisingly revealed
that smoked pianos
sound nobler than cooked ones
In huge fireplaces
they now hang
those dispensers of musical delight
like blackened hams
before
smokey-grey and spicy
they satisfy the cognoscenti
Henceforth
the famous house of Bösenstein
will refrain
from boiling pianos hard or soft
according to taste

The Sicilian pygmy elephants
have resurfaced
In single file
they roam
trunk to tail
the catacombs of Palermo

Their comeback
after five hundred thousand years
has given the Sicilian pianoforte industry
a second wind
The so-called Clayderman Grand
which allows even children and matrons
to play sixths with one finger
appears destined
to undermine the ivory business

The discovery of opposites
has already rocked Paradise
On our stages
it has become a daily occurrence
Surrounded by naked women and beer-cans
Florestan delights in his dungeon
Pushed by Leporello
Don Giovanni travels Spain in a wheelchair
A pink-skinned Othello
murders black Desdemona
In the face of such calamity
what else can we do
but pronounce right away
the opposite of what we wish to say
thus giving directors a chance
to perpetrate
without any loss of face
if not in pristine innocence
the opposite's opposite

Where those laughing angels
could have emerged from
remains obscure
Unfit for singing
they appear to some of us
devils in disguise
if not downright human
Others
see them as children
who never learnt to be wise
giggling
in the face of a threatening world
unfeeling like gods

On an island
remote from all geography
between unicorns and basilisks
the last angels dwell
higher beings
who had failed to notice
that the spirit no longer blew
Earnestly
they admonish grieve play music
beckoning us to follow their trail
grow seraphic
climb rungless ladders
to reach a deserted heaven
a theatre abandoned by its stage-hands
a rigging-loft
unrigged